Be a Badass Godde

MW01492937

Dedication

This book is dedicated to all the remarkable people in my life, especially my beautiful amazing children, Talitha, Daisha, and Gabriel. My journey to appreciating what a goddess is began with your love igniting my inner flame into the inferno it remains to be to this day. As the years pass by, and they will - this will serve as my guide for you now and when I am breathless, living only in your memories. May you find comfort within, realizing you, too are a badass god/dess.

INTRODUCTION

MIND

FINDING MY MOTIVATION

KEEPING MY DREAMS ALIVE

BODY

OWINING IT

LIVING IT

SPIRIT

UNIVERSAL CONNECTION

IMMERSION

ACKNOWLEDGMENTS

NOTES

REFERENCES

Introduction

Hello beautiful soul! Congratulations on taking the proverbial plunge into a magical journey taking charge of your life: mind, body, and spirit. I will be sharing with you my own journey and what tools I use to exceptionally level up my own life! I realized that if I wanted a better life, I was going to have to make some changes and, in this book, I've outlined them for you. Now you don't have to spend years of trial and error to get the same results (wink). Please use my failures and successes as your field guide.

My personal goals are listed below and I'm guessing your "why" list contains a few of the same goals. Achieving my goals thru trial and error on my roller-coaster journey for holistic knowledge and success has lighted a beacon so bright that you too can find your way thru the dark. Echo it with your own journey using the simple lifestyle hacks in this workbook! My journey is lifelong venture and will continue to evolve and grow.

Speaking from personal experience I never found a single resource that met all of my needs holistically. My decision to celebrate my journey by creating this workbook is to accomplish that for you and scream from the roof tops what I know to be a fantastic way of life! We all dream of finding something we are passionate about and sharing it, this is mine. I spent too many years hurting – I didn't need to and you shouldn't either! I did not need a complicated manual and neither do you, this is simple and meant to be – don't overcomplicate the process!

- ✓ Deep Spiritual Connection

- ✓ Healthy Loving Relationships

- ✓ Substantial Health Improvement

- ✓ Genuine Poise & Positive Self-image

- ✓ Career Fulfillment

- ✓ Financial Well-being

Now get to it, be the badass goddess you were meant to be

and own it!

Finding My Motivation

"You are just as worthy, deserving, and capable of creating and sustaining extraordinary health, wealth, happiness, love, and success in your life, as any other person on earth."

— Hal Elrod

"In life you need either inspiration or desperation."

– Tony Robbins

I'd like to tell you how easy it was to get my life on track but, I REALLY had to dig DEEP on some of my darkest days, reminding myself that I owed it to yours truly. It takes courage to stand at the threshold alone, look in the mirror and love yourself exactly as you are. Sigh…I've spent so long wanting to be more like everyone else: prettier, skinnier, smarter, richer, funnier, popular, etc. because I believed that it would make me whole, feel loved and complete. I stood in the mirror every evening and every morning staring into the reflection learning to love every version of myself: past, present and future. Holding myself accountable was something new, I had only reserved that unpleasantry for others (giggling). With that being said, I was desperate to feel restored physically and mentally. My soul hurt; I was in catastrophic despair.

In the spring of 2017 for many reasons my marriage had disintegrated. Sometimes no matter what you do to hold it together it isn't enough and you need to consider that it is time for change even when it's scary as hell. I was suddenly a single parent of three children, homeless, morbidly obese, faithless, estranged from my family and hurting so profoundly it rocked my very core. I was so deeply wounded and living on autopilot going thru the motions to achieve survival. If you are hurting and it feels like all the oxygen is being sucked out of the room, I urge you to remember that no matter how frightening and painful it is **it won't last forever**.

To put things into perspective and set the stage I'll let you peek under the sheets of what it was like during those mind, body, and spirit numbing months. I woke up one morning in early spring of 2017 and took my oldest daughter for her driving test and as I stood on the side of the road alone waiting for her to complete the test I started crying and knew with every fiber of my being that I had to start over. That afternoon I picked up my other two children from school, drove to Walmart to buy a tent and never went home again.

Yes, you read that correctly. I did say bought a tent. We camped for months in NY in the rain and snow and stayed with a few friends for a night or two. When you are sleeping with your children in freezing temperatures with towels around the tent to collect the condensation and waking up wet from it dripping all over the sleeping bags trust me it's hard to see the silver lining.

One evening it was so cold I grabbed the kids, our blankets and we slept in the car running the heat…all I could hear was our teeth chattering. There was a terrible thunderstorm knocking down trees that tore up our camp site aka makeshift home so horribly that the campground moved us into a cabin for a few nights free of charge – another very low point for me. Hands down the single memory that we all laugh about still to this day is the morning that I was held hostage in the bathroom by a garter snake until the park ranger came to relocate it outside! Just thinking about this still makes me laugh out loud, it was not funny at the time!

05.05.17 Campsite Thunderstorm→

There were many nights I was not sure how much longer I could hold it together. I spent countless nights alone standing in the campground shower with tears streaming down my face to hide my despair from the kids. I had to go to work and continue to function as if nothing was wrong…this was rock bottom for me.

That being said, I also remember some of the most kindhearted souls who helped us without us asking. We had people open their homes, cook meals, free automotive work, cash…literally cash from a teenage young man to feed us –

there are amazing souls out there that saved us in ways they will never understand even to this day. In our darkest hours we are shown light if we choose to have appreciation for it. It changes your soul when you do. I had to find a way to make our lives good again. I reluctantly withdrew a loan from my retirement to get us into a small one-bedroom apartment. It was a shock to me that I was required to have my husbands' signature to take a loan from my own retirement, so displeased with that little tidbit. The one-bedroom apartment was ridiculously small and overpriced, but it was warm, dry and ours. It felt so good to sleep on the carpeted floor that first night I will never forget it! Watching the children fall asleep on the warm carpeted floor in total serenity and joy after what we had endured was enough to keep me going. As grateful as I was for the glimmer of light and improved conditions, I really was broken inside in a way that words just can't describe.

By the fall of that year my life began to stabilize and the emotional flood from that year's events that I was mentally numb to, irrevocably rushed in like a violent ocean all at once. You can't hold back the ocean forever. One evening late after the kids went to sleep, I slid slowly down onto the floor next to my bed alone and just cried, and cried, and cried some more. I was so defeated that night. Even now the words to describe my emotional collapse still render me breathless. I decided that evening in my despair that I had to do something drastic to get my life back! It did not take years to change direction, in that precise moment the course of my life changed forever. I know that what it takes to change a life is a single moment in time, a single choice can change the course of the future, and it did.

Over twenty years earlier an extended family member bestowed me with a copy of The Power of Your Subconscious Mind by Joseph Murphy and scribed inside was a note "Jenny - this changed my life". I did what any nineteen-year-old does...I skimmed it and thought I got what I needed. Apparently, I knew everything there was to know about life already.

With my recent separation and moving, most of my belongings were in boxes in a storage unit just a little bigger than a closet or in a dumpster - for the life of me I could not find the book that I had been gifted all those years ago. Determined, I embarked on a hunt and started searching online to get my hands on another copy. However, I could not remember the name of it! I first came across The Miracle Morning by Hal Elrod purely by astonishing dumb luck and I am so grateful I did...it literally saved my life that night and set in motion my personal journey to becoming one badass goddess! From that moment on my hunger for knowledge and personal growth has run wild. I didn't invent any new practices; I replicated everything I could get my hands on until I found what really works. Elizabeth López thank you

Stella / Be a Badass Goddess & Own it!

for the beautiful gift you gave me, it was so much more than

a book and it changed my life too!

~HEALING SOURCE~

Chalice of Isis - Goddess of magic and wisdom, she was said to be cleverer than a million gods.

List (3) three constructive books you are committed to reading AND **start #1 this week**!

01)_____

02)_____

03)_____

Stella / Be a Badass Goddess & Own it!

Jenny's →

#1 the Miracle Morning by Hal Elrod

#2 The Secret by Rhonda Byrne

#3 The Power of Your Subconscious Mind by Joseph
Murphy, PH.D., D.D.

#4 Think & Grow Rich by Napoleon Hill

#5 the Magic by Rhonda Byrne

#4 Unleash Your Inner Money Babe by Kathrin Zenkina

<u>Chalice of Kuan Yin</u> - <u>Her name translates to "perceiving</u>

<u>the sounds (or cries) of the world." She is a Goddess of</u>

<u>mercy, dedicated to relieving the suffering in the world.</u>

List your top (3) three reasons, what's driving you?

01)_____

02)_____

03)_____

Stella / Be a Badass Goddess & Own it!

Jenny's →

#1 Deep Spiritual Connection

#2 Healthy Loving Relationships

#3 Substantial Health Improvement

#4 Genuine Poise & Positive Self-image

#5 Career Fulfillment

#6 Financial Well-being

Keeping Dreams Alive

"Always remember that where you are is a result of who you were, but where you go depends entirely on who you choose to be, from this moment on."

- Hal Elrod

"The greater danger for most of us isn't that our aim is too high and miss it, but that it is too low and we reach it."

- Michelangelo

This is the sequence of events that took place allowing me to identify what was most important in my life. Prioritizing what dreams I desperately wanted to become my reality. In life the best way to replicate a recipe is to have a clear understanding of the ingredients and in what order they are integrated. This is my formula for holistic improvement and just like a recipe **the elements and sequence are essential to duplicating the results**.

I jumped into my transformation like a sugar cube in hot coffee, in a state of complete surrender. I immersed myself with an iron resolve, life was going to get better! I read the Miracle Morning by Hal Elrod cover to cover that weekend. I <u>did not</u> skim thru the pages I processed every single word - you know what I mean… yellow highlighter, glitter gel pen underlining, page corner folding, stars, circles, note taking, yeah…sigh…that kind of reading. The following weeks were consumed with YouTube videos and audibles by Hal Elrod, Tony Robbins, and Jim Rohn to name a few of the absolute best in my opinion. I can't recall how, but I also stumbled across another book Unleash your Inner Money Babe by Kathrin Zenkina which was crucial to my journey on understanding my financial health, it is also where I was introduced to The Secret by Rhonda Byrne and that my friends was the fuel that powered my transformation!

Remember this is a workbook and you need to do the work - so absolutely mark it up and make it a beautiful mess and get a notebook to write down what resonates with you, do whatever works for you to make a connection – like your life depends on it!

Throughout this process I've read many, many, many books and still do to this day. In addition, I began journaling daily, created my "goals" list, vision boards, and on an elemental level got to know myself while unveiling my reasons and goals. I learned to love myself and my life going thru this evolution. I certainly had not realized just how intensely I was wounded until I began healing and truly learned how to love the woman and badass goddess I am today! I did not deteriorate in a day and did not rebuild in a day either so easy does it, **you are worth it and you will get there too**! I literally followed every recommendation in books, programs, and forced myself every single day to give 110% even when I did not want to and would tell myself "suck it up buttercup, you can do this dam it" …and you know what I could and I did…you can and will too!

Brick by brick I began rebuilding myself from the inside out. I focused on progress, not perfection and many times had to take more than a few steps backwards to propel me leaps and bounds ahead so anticipate this and understand it is still success if you don't quit! One of my early projects of self-healing, "Mirror Magick" that I did with my kids was and still is my favorite because of the reflective impact it had. I repeat this at least once annually even to this day! I also still to this day have times that I get discouraged and feel that negative self-talk funk sneaking up on me and IMMEDIATELY recognize it and watch a YouTube motivational video. I am continually rewiring my brain to stop that shit!

~HEALING SOURCE~

Chalice of Aphrodite - The most beautiful deity whose angelic appearance could charm even the hardest of hearts, she possessed the title of goddess of beauty, love, and desire.

Create your Mirror Magick: I used dollar store sticky notes and markers for ours. Write on each one a word or two that captures your inner divine and stick them up in your room around your mirror or in the bathroom so you see them every single day. You can Google ideas and pictures of this, it is being utilized in schools, businesses, homes, etc.

☼ Ideas: Motivational Messages, Compliments, Goals, Reminders:

- o You got this!
- o Make yourself a priority!
- o Decide, commit, succeed!
- o Be the energy you want to attract!
- o My story isn't over yet!
- o Do epic shit!
- o Count your blessings!
- o Live with a grateful heart!
- o Refuse to lose!
- o You are beautiful!
- o Look for the beauty in everyone!
- o Don't get sidetracked by people who are off track!
- o You are what someone looks forward to!
- o Shine bright like a diamond!
- o Crush Your Workout!
- o Yes, you can!

- o Your day will go the corners of your mouth turn, smile!

- o Be Yourself!

- o Chin up buttercup!

- o Today is a great day to have a great day!

- o Failure is not an option!

Chalice of Sekhmet - Sekhmet is the lioness goddess of the Egyptian Pantheon, a fierce protector of truth, balance, and the Cosmic order of Ma'at. She represents the transformative power of kundalini energy, or sekhem, and is the main goddess to harness this power for healing.

List your goals under these categories to get started and be specific: people, places, things, feelings, hopes, dreams, small, medium, large, etc. – DIG DEEP HERE!!

Badass Goddess Blueprint Grid

Health & Body	Relationships	Personal Desires
Career/Work	Finances "Money"	Material Things
Knowledge	Miscellaneous	Spirituality

Jenny's →

Health & Body	Relationships	Personal Desires
a) Love the current version of myself and take pride it!	a) Unbreakable bond of love, respect, and joy with my children	a) Reiki mastery and personal practice
b) Quality meditation and sleep schedule	b) Peace of mind and healed relationships with my parents to mirror mine with my own children	b) Raise my frequency thru gratitude and grace
c) Healthy eating and sustainable exercise routine		c) Get "skinny" enough to zipline, parasail, rollercoaster, fly to Hawaii, and go horseback riding
d) Weight = 140 pounds	c) To feel the love, healing, kind, genuine, deep emotional connection to my soulmate – the kind that overflows your cup	d) Memorialize my weight loss journey with a tattoo for every 10 pounds. Living in the here and now
e) Healthy teeth, pain free joints, get 1st mammogram		

Career/Work	Finances "Money"	Material Things
a) Make a difference	a) Always have more than enough and extra	a) Black Mercedes AMG E 53 Sedan
b) Feel appreciated and respected	b) Be generous and kind	b) Brick Mediterranean style home near water, with a fireplace, firepit, jacuzzi, pool, master bedroom with ensuite, and a separate room for each kid!
c) Feel fulfilled and love what I do stress free.	c) Show my children how beautiful life is and give them the best of it	
d) Be an amazing leader and sharpen my skills	d) Take amazing vacations	
e) Salary 110K – 150K	e) Not have to look at my bank account to go shopping	

Knowledge	Miscellaneous	Spirituality
a) Be open minded	a) Set new goals regularly	a) Find what's right for me
b) Be happy you know you don't know everything	b) Don't fear failure	b) Make a deep connection that I can physically and mentally feel
c) Stay hungry	c) Find your reset button and use it when needed	

29

Stella / Be a Badass Goddess & Own it!

Chalice of Gaea/Gaia - Gaea is not just the earth goddess in Greek mythology, but the actual Earth as well. In Greek myth, she gives birth to the sky and sea, as well as all of the Titans and Giants.

Take the time to create a vision board now and look at it every morning and evening! You can do this on poster board, your laptop, a smartphone app, etc. you get the idea!! I personally loved the good old-fashioned poster board for $1 and included my children in on the fun! I printed a very random beach entrance picture from the internet as one of the images on my very first vision board, 45 days later the photo below was taken at a Florida beach I had never seen photos of or ever visited…now that's manifesting power! In fact, that was my first trip to Florida ever!

- ✓ Get some supplies: magazines, glues ticks, stickers, ribbon, etc.

- ✓ Create Sacred Space: put on some inspirational music, play a motivational YouTube video in the background, set the stage

- ✓ Find your images + words

- ✓ If they resonate with your vision, then paste them to the page

- ✓ Put your vision board somewhere that you can see it, look at it every morning and evening

- ✓ Many of your "Badass Goddess Blueprint Grid" items should be on this

- ✓ Raise your awareness to any internal resistance and remind yourself thoughts are things!!

Owning It

"Your will has to be stronger than your excuses. Your will has to be stronger than your fear."

— Bryant McGill

"Take care of your body. It's the only place you have to live."

– Jim Rohn

I had become a master of overcomplicating my health. My health slowly deteriorated and over the years I replayed so many excuses that I honestly started to believe them slowly killing myself. I was raised in a family that was morbidly obese and we celebrated everything in life with food from holidays, birthdays, life events, every outing was celebrated with food and you know pizza Wednesday's (giggle) and that's just how life was as a kid. Keep in mind I was 120 pounds soaking wet as a teenager - I was not negatively impacted or scared as a youth. I believe that our parents do the best they can with the life tools they have in hand at the time.

On a subconscious level my childhood introduced to me that food was a feel-good commodity and a happiness accessory. I don't know when exactly but as I moved into adulthood, I certainly made a mental connection that yummy food was like taking a breath of fresh air when I was tired, stressed, lonely, and bored. In those moments I found comfort like a warm blanket feels on a cold winter night.

Now remember, all of my immediate family members are morbidly obese, too, so I'm no stranger to the vicious cycles that occur, and I've seen the long-term damage emotionally, physically, and the spiritual toll that it takes. I had created my own story that I told myself too and it kept me in a state of constant physical chaos...and I chose to believe that story for many years. It was like night and day when I decided to make a change, there was no half measures to be had, I flipped the switch and never looked back. My will to break the cycle for me and my children was and still is stronger than all my excuses and fears combined!

I again did a little digging you could say, I watched countless hours of infomercials, YouTube videos, pod casts, and read articles on health & fitness to gain a better understanding of the mechanics of not only weight loss but overall anatomy and health. What I found was misleading, degrading, unachievable, and overall depressing how little the mainstream really understands the mind body connection. I have seen all the gimmicks and programs that my own family has tried and it's no wonder they didn't work. Everyone seemingly has an opinion and different method that they believe is a fantastic fix that saved someone in their circle that they now want to sell to the world.

I wanted and demanded more from the experience than just getting a summer beach body and wearing smaller clothes, I wanted a phenomenal transformation from the inside out. I wanted the change to be deeply ingrained into the fabric of my being. I knew it could not be a cookie cutter diet with any single plan out there. I understood I was going to have to derive a blueprint with segments from various recipes, programs, and concepts but not everything from a single one of them. I began experimenting to figure out what I did and did not like with the understanding that it was not to lose weight. It was just to start building my "I like this" healthy food list. I'm a picky eater and if it doesn't taste good, I'm not eating it twice.

I refused to diet and still do to this day! I knew already that diets in the traditional sense do not work long term. I chose to create a list of foods that I loved to eat that happen to also be good for me and began swapping the poorly chosen ones. You'll notice there is no elimination, I do not have a "I can't eat that" list – that is the ultimate hell no for me! I do however, substitute healthy mouthwatering meals in place of fast food 95% of the time now.

This Anonymous quote really hit home for me "Anyone can work out for an hour, but to control what goes on your plate the other 23 hours…. that's hard work!" and it just clicked for me – challenge accepted! The specific timing of eating was important for me as much as what I was eating. I rarely was eating breakfast or lunch and if I did it was grossly over a healthy caloric value. Prior to this evaluation and implementation 95% of my daily caloric intake was in the evening before bed between 7PM and 10PM.

I had to experiment with what worked best for **my life**, **my schedule** and **my body**. It's great that there are recommendations out there. However, they have specific content, times, volumes, calories, etc. That is not realistic for me. It's not how I want to live my life on a stopwatch out of a daily planner…that's depressing to me – that overcomplicates unnecessarily. For once ignore your coworker's, family, friends, and even strangers' opinions and do what you know is right for you not what they think is right for you. "Opinions are like assholes, everybody's got one and everyone thinks everyone else's stinks." — Simone Elkeles

~HEALING SOURCE~

Chalice of Ixcacao - Goddess of chocolate. Ixcacao (or, Cacao Woman) was a Mayan and Meso-American goddess of fertility and agriculture (and, of course, chocolate).

Find your to (10) ten (or more) "Wow I like this!" list of healthy substitutes using the four qualifiers below to guide you. Now get to experimenting, there are no limits!

- ✪ Look & Taste = awesome
- ✪ Calories = low
- ✪ Quality = nutrient rich
- ✪ Preparation = not expert level

Stella / Be a Badass Goddess & Own it!

01)_____

02)_____

03)_____

04)_____

05)_____

06)_____

07)_____

08)_____

09)_____

10)_____

Jenny's →

#	Recipe / Item	Source	Craving / Substitute
1	Frozen Banana & Cacao Smoothie Recipe	elizabethrider.com	Ice Cream
2	Monk fruit Sweetener *tip: use in coffee & cooking	Walmart (Online)	Sugar
3	Bomba Burgers	Keto Comfort Foods by Maria Emmerich	Double Cheeseburger
4	Chili Cheese Dog Casserole *tip: mix in cubed mug bread 🌀	Keto Comfort Foods by Maria Emmerich	Cheese Dog
5	Pepperoni and Chicken Pizza Bake	The I Love My Air Fryer Keto Diet Recipe Book	Pizza
6	Southern Fried Chicken	The I Love My Air Fryer Keto Diet Recipe Book	Deep Fried Chicken
7	Keto Stuffed Bacon Wrapped Chicken	mooreorlesscooking.com	Hands Down Any Chicken Dinner 🌀
8	Paleo Chicken and Broccoli	realfoodwithjessica.com	Local Chinese Chicken and Broccoli take out
9	Slow Cooker Curried Chicken & Cabbage	thecheerfulkitchen.com	Local Jamaican take out
10	Taco Salad	wholesomeyum.com	Local Taco take out

Chalice of Sirona - In eastern Gaul, Sirona was honored as a deity of healing springs and waters. Sirona's temples were often constructed on or near thermal springs and healing wells.

Okay now it's time for you to GTS (Google That Shit) and you will find some awesome things that are really important for you to understand about your body. These are the top topics that I googled and find fascinating – feel empowered to go beyond these! Please keep in mind I'm not a professional (there are enough of those), this is my expedition to real and successful weight loss to help guide you on yours. I do not follow any single plan 100% and this exercise is only to have a better understanding of the hybrid version that I use by understanding the basic elements. I read a post on Facebook that suits my life "70% Keto, 20% Low Carb, 10% Living Wild".

✪ Ketosis

- Ketosis is a normal process that happens when your body doesn't have enough carbs to burn for energy. Instead, it burns fat and makes substances called ketones, which it can use for fuel.

✪ Intermittent Fasting

- "RESTRICTED EATING WINDOW - The other approach that's commonly included in discussions of intermittent fasting is the restricted eating window. I talked about this in my episode on timing your meals. Instead of restricting your food intake, you restrict your meal schedule.

  Again, there are lots of variations on this approach. Some people follow a four-hour eating window, essentially eating just one meal a day. Others might eat two or three meals within an eight- or ten-hour window. (If you're a breakfast skipper, you might already be doing this without even realizing it!)."

✪ Body Type Physique Classifications

    o   Ectomorph: "A human physical type (somatotype) <u>tending toward linearity</u>, as determined by the physique-classification system developed by the American psychologist W.H. Sheldon. Although classification by the Sheldon system is not absolute, a person is classed as an ectomorph if ectomorphy predominates over endomorphy and mesomorphy in his body build. *The extreme ectomorph has a thin face with high forehead and receding chin; narrow chest and abdomen; a narrow heart; rather long, thin arms and legs; little body fat and little muscle; but a large skin surface and a large nervous system.* If well fed, he does not gain weight easily; if he becomes fat, he is still considered an ectomorph, only overweight. Compare endomorph; mesomorph."

o Mesomorph: "A human physical type (somatotype) that is <u>marked by greater than average muscular development</u>, as determined by the physique-classification system developed by American psychologist W.H. Sheldon. Although the Sheldon system of classification does not make absolute distinctions between types, a person is classed as a mesomorph if mesomorphy predominates over endomorphy and ectomorphy in his body build. *The extreme mesomorph has a square, massive head; broad, muscular chest and shoulders; a large heart; heavily muscled arms and legs; and minimal body fat. He tends to develop muscle easily.* His muscular development can usually be distinguished from that of one who has developed his muscles through body-building exercises."

o   Endomorph: "A human physical type (somatotype) <u>tending toward roundness,</u> as determined by the physique-classification system developed by American psychologist W.H. Sheldon. *The extreme endomorph has a body as nearly globular as humanly possible; he has a round head, a large, round abdomen, large internal organs relative to his size, rather short arms and legs with fat upper arms and thighs, but slender wrists and ankles.* Under normal conditions the endormorphic individual has a great deal of body fat, but he is not simply a fat person; if starved, he remains an endomorph, only thinner."

- ✪ Low Carbohydrate

  - ○ "A very-low-carb diet must be high in fat. Otherwise, you won't get enough energy or nutrition to sustain yourself.

  - ○ If you want to get into ketosis and reap the full metabolic benefits of low-carb diets, going under 50 grams of carbs per day may be necessary.

  - ○ Excessive protein consumption on a low-carb diet can prevent you from getting into ketosis.

  - ○ Low-carb diets lower insulin levels, making your kidneys excrete excess sodium. This can lead to a mild sodium deficiency."

✪ Recommended rate for weight loss

    o "A weight loss of one to two pounds a week is the typical recommendation. Although that may seem like a slow pace for weight loss, it's more likely to help you maintain your weight loss for the long term.

    o Remember that one pound (0.45 kilogram) of fat contains 3,500 calories. So, to lose one pound a week, you need to burn 500 more calories than you eat each day (500 calories x 7 days = 3,500 calories)."

✪ Carb Cycling

    o Carb cycling involves planned increases and decreases in carbohydrate intake depending on the day. While a high-carb day calls for eating

2 to 2.5 grams of carbs per pound of body weight, a low-carb day includes approximately 0.5 grams of carbs per pound of body weight. There is also a no-carb day that usually calls for less than 30 grams of carbohydrates. Carb cycling allows you to still eat carbs from clean sources, and cycling enables you to better utilize fat for burning as fuel, as opposed to burning carbs and muscle tissue for fuel.

Stella / Be a Badass Goddess & Own it!

<u>Jenny's Schedule→</u>

Most Days [5 - 7 depending on the week]. You do have to leave some room to live a little "wink", keeping in mind moderation. <u>Eat healthy snacks when you are hungry.</u>

KEEP IT SIMPLE we know exactly what goes in cannot exceed what we are using to fuel our temples each day!

- Breakfast:

    - Badass Goddess Coffee (Coffee, MCT Powder, Creamer, Monk Fruit)

- Lunch

    - 16 oz Water

    - Almonds

    - 8 oz Dietary Supplement Lemon Flavor Drink (sugar free)

- Meal Replacement Shake Chocolate Rich in MCTs, 1 tbsp of PBfit All-Natural Peanut Butter Powder, Powdered Peanut Spread from Real Roasted Pressed Peanuts, 4g of Protein (1/2 serving)

- Dinner

    - One of my "Wow I like this" list of recipes. This list grows weekly as I find new things that I love! 😊

Living It

"If you want something you've never had, you must be willing to do something you've never done."

— Thomas Jefferson

"Keep your mind fixed on what you want in life: not on what you don't want."

- Napoleon Hill

Ah, now this no doubt was the most challenging part of my journey and the most frustrating in the beginning. I tried many fitness routines only to have them end in excruciating pain, injury, and embarrassment causing me to do one thing—consistently. Stop and need to restart. For anyone 250 + pounds you know exactly what I mean…most fitness video routines are not made for fat people--they are made to maintain being skinny! Grr is how I felt after watching what seemed like the millionth fitness video that was not even remotely in my possibility of physical abilities. I was willing to push myself to extremes, but these were just absurd and super not realistic in my starting physique. Sigh...this was devastating for me to accept that this was my starting point, it was my own personal walk of shame and likely what kept me there for so long.

I searched for a basic (emphasizing "basic") weight routine (5 pounds) that I could do start to finish. It was honestly so embarrassing that I started in the early mornings and usually alone - it was way more difficult than I anticipated just to get thru a simple routine. There was not a single one that I could do without modifying at least one (usually more) of the moves. At that time, I could not get on the floor and get back up to do ANY floor exercises and bending my knees was almost out of the question with severe joint pain. I absolutely refused to believe that this hell was going to also be my future reality! I did not quit, instead I found alternatives.

This, too, sparked hours of online research on fitness programs, workouts, videos, articles, dance, you name it if I found it then I investigated it! I was really taken back by what I found more than I can express in this workbook. This is when I felt my first real blow to my motivation in transforming my life. I was faced with the reality that this was going to be a challenge for real. Each person faces different mountains that they must overcome and this my friends was mine. I can vividly remember typing into YouTube "workouts for morbidly obese" and it just made me cry. You know what? Sometimes we need a good crying to clean out our emotional volcanos to start with a positive, fertile mental mind frame.

After all the tears, I took in a deep breath and made a video on my laptop talking to myself, **"I accept that every journey begins with a single step and moment in time,**

this is mine". Each and every time that I start to slack in my efforts, I remind myself of that day and it's like jet fuel for me. Find what fuels your fire and remind yourself often. I was determined to make my transformation fun to overcome the sinking feeling I started with and involved my children when possible. We turned my before pictures into a photo shoot, filling the event with giggles and movie star poses. This was much less painful and showed my children and I that it's important to love who we are every step of the way.

The first time I worked up the guts to get on the rowing machine at the gym after my daughter kept prodding me for weeks was like climbing Mount Everest and the feeling was amazing. It seems silly now how fearful I was of people seeing me at the gym working out because of my size. I did get glares of judgement and pity. But I did not own their insecurities. I will not feel ashamed of working on my hopes and dreams ever again! When I see someone working hard at making their lives better, I smile at them, knowing how much courage it takes and I also know that a small gesture of kindness means so much. Now I keep setting goals and focus on crushing them, instead of on who's watching or what they think!

Stella / Be a Badass Goddess & Own it!

~HEALING SOURCE~

Chalice of Nike - Nike is the Goddess of strength, speed, and victory.

Find (5) ways you can incorporate physical fitness into your life, be specific don't let yourself off the hook here! You want a variety so you can rotate them to match your mood.

*Reminder: 30 minutes = 2% of your day = no excuses!

01)_____

02)_____

03)_____

Stella / Be a Badass Goddess & Own it!

04)_____

05)_____

Stella / Be a Badass Goddess & Own it!

Jenny's Favorites →

#1 Fitbit, set a daily 10,000-step goal

#2 Gym membership 10,10,10 routine: elliptical, rowing, treadmill

#3 Free Workout for Obese / Overweight from Beachfitrob.com and Beachbody, the P90X People video on YouTube

#4 HASfit videos on YouTube

#5 The Fitness Marshall on YouTube

#6 Cycling, on a local trail with my inexpensive "girly beach cruiser" bike (no gears) with my children

#7 Walking

Chalice of Asclepius - A Greek God who is honored by healers and physicians. He is known as the God of medicine, and his serpent-draped staff, The Rod of Asclepius, is still found as a symbol of medical practice today. Honored by doctors, nurses and scientists alike.

Find your starting point and draw your line in the sand, make your mark and go! I personally found that tracking my progress every month kept me accountable and let me celebrate my success propelling my forward movement!

Measurements →

- ➢ Weight (lb) _____

- ➢ Chest (in) _____

- ➢ Waist (in) _____

- ➢ Hips (in) _____

- ➢ Wrist (in) _____

Stella / Be a Badass Goddess & Own it!

> ➢ Forearm (in) _____

> ➢ Bicep (in) _____

> ➢ Thigh (in) _____

Spirit

Universal Connection

"Have you ever lost yourself in a kiss? I mean pure psychedelic inebriation. Not just lustful petting but transcendental metamorphosis when you became aware that the greatness of this being was breathing into you. Licking the sides and corners of your mouth, like sealing a thousand fleshy envelopes filled with the essence of your passionate being and then opened by the same mouth and delivered back to you, over and over again - the first kiss of the rest of your life. A kiss that confirms that the universe is aligned, that the world's greatest resource is love, and maybe even that God is a woman. With or without a belief in God, all kisses are metaphors decipherable by allocations of time, circumstance, and understanding"

— Saul Williams

"I change my life when I change my thinking.

I am Light. I am Spirit.

I am a wonderful, capable being.

And it is time for me to acknowledge

that I create my own reality with my thoughts.

If I want to change my reality,

then it is time for me to change my mind."

— Louise L. Hay

I will begin by stating that I do not claim any one religion, practice or belief, but I find truth in them all. In my extended family there are many ordained ministers and no lack of very rigid judgmental beliefs. Perhaps this is what spurred me to reject a single ideal to be the only "right" one. Instead of continuing to emphasize what I did not believe by forced conformity, I refocused on connecting with what resonated with my spirit. In the darkest hours of my life I found the quiet in the storm, meditation. The daily practice of incorporating mindfulness allowed me to own just my spiritual needs and stop stuffing 50lbs of inherited shit into a 5lb bag on my back.

It was refreshing to acknowledge that not a single person is without imperfection. Honestly, it's what makes us beautiful. My experience did not take me around the globe in my ventures to learn more about spiritual beliefs and practices, it did open my eyes that many spiritual practices vibrated to my very soul's beat. The feeling of making that beautiful connection being sensitive to the overwhelming love frequency was and is still like waves crashing into my existence. This was so profound it brought me to tears. [A1]

This fundamental feeling of fulfillment, connection and grounding lead me to continue to keep an open mind. I do not have to adopt others beliefs should I chose not to and neither do you. In my personal experience, even in my extended family those that hide behind the armor of their faith, utter daggers of judgement, and gush with self-importance are simply in need of their own healing and projecting – do not carry their burdens as yours. The ability to stop for a single moment in time and align to the universal frequency that connects us is pure magick. To find my personal true north I kept a completely open mind and ignored everything I had been taught to gain knowledge and achieve what my spirit craved. After almost forty years of being an empty chalice - I found my fountain.

~HEALING SOURCE~

Chalice of Mayet - A female goddess in the ancient Egyptian religion who represented truth, justice, balance and morality. The daughter of the Egyptian sun deity Ra and wife of the moon god Thoth, she served a kind of spirit of justice to the Egyptians. She decided whether a person would successfully reach the afterlife, by weighing their soul against her feather of truth, and was the personification of the cosmic order and a representation of the stability of the universe.

Find (5) practices to research and unlearn bias, expanding your stance to open yourself to endless possibilities of spiritual abundance. Being open to learning what others believe and practice does not mean that you will be tainted or that you have to adopt them as your beliefs. This will serve only to remove the need for brick walls forged in fear of the unknown, and you may find along the way truths you never fathomed in the realm of probability. Being the proverbial black sheep, I focused on exploring the social taboo's via videos, books, groups, etc. seeking to understand each. I was determined to see beyond the religious perspectives and dig deep into the associated science and histories.

01)_____

02)_____

03)_____

04)_____

05)_____

Stella / Be a Badass Goddess & Own it!

Jenny's →

#1 Christianity

#2 Paganism

#3 Buddhism

#4 Astrology

#5 Divination

#6 Auras, Chakras, Reiki

#7 Telepathy, Telekinesis, Teleportation

#8 Herbalism

#9 Shamanism

#10 Aromatherapy & Apothecary Practice's

Immersion

"Intuition is really a sudden immersion of the soul into the universal current of life."

- Paulo Coelho

"A monk is simply a traveler, except the journey is inwards."

— Jay Shetty

At the conclusion of my initial quest for a deeper meaning in my life it hit me like a tidal wave that what I had been searching for was always there within me. I was so focused on finding it somewhere else that I overlooked the storehouse within. My spiritual awaking was an amazingly beautiful journey that I promise myself I will never cease to explore. In our daily existence we immerse ourselves in the mundane routines, opinions, and dreams of others - why not completely immerse ourselves in our own hopes, dreams, love and compassion? It really is that simple, like so many aspects of our lives we overcomplicate having a spiritual connection. My perspective shift has opened so many doors I didn't realize were even there!

The moment I chose to see life thru a different lens everything changed for me. I am in awe of so many brilliant trailblazers there are out there. Find your tribe. They do exist! I absolutely love this quote by Confucius, "If you are the smartest person in the room, then you are in the wrong room." This makes me giggle, having a recent recollection of being asked in a professional setting to refrain from contributing in hopes of fostering the groups development – I knew in that exact moment I was in the wrong room! Find your personal nirvana and totally immerse yourself in making life as amazing as possible – find that childhood wonder that somewhere along the way was lost and dust it off! Stop lowering the bar for others when you find yourself in the wrong room.

Years later I am a Reiki Master, manage an apothecary, maintain a mindful practice of self-love, maintain a daily meditation routine, keep a gratitude list, serve a social media group, exercise regularly living a healthy life and fulfill a positive role in my children's lives. I healed my strained familial bonds and continue to forgive transgressions mending them a little more each day. With my own growth I am now able to open my heart to loving and being loved again. Nothing is lost forever. Set healthy boundaries and anything is possible. Now it's your turn to join me and jump into the rest of your life and make it exceed all your wildest expectations.

Own it and embody all that you are in your mind, body, and spirit standing firm knowing you are a badass goddess!

Chalice of Oya - She is the Goddess of thunder, lightning, tornadoes, winds, rainstorms and hurricanes. A Fire Goddess, it is Oya who brings rapid change and aids us in both inner and outer transformation.

What (5) things are you incorporating into the "new version" of your life?

01)_____

02)_____

03)_____

04)_____

05)_____

Stella / Be a Badass Goddess & Own it!

Jenny's →

#1 Listen to a motivational YouTube video every morning while journaling

#2 Listen to an evening mediational every evening

#3 Get exercise 3-5 days a week

#4 Eat for the life you love

#5 List 5 things you are grateful for every morning

Acknowledgements

My life's journey from rock bottom to the summit has been an amazing journey and was fueled by so many events and people that it is challenging to capture them all individually. I would like to take this opportunity to highlight a few that were the most profound. I am so grateful that you are a part of my life past, present, or future.

❖ Elizabeth – The spark of inspiration.

❖ Gabriel, Daisha, and Talitha – An unbreakable bond of faith, hope, and love thru any storm!

❖ Boris – My beautiful soulmate you understood the sacrifices we made to heal our hearts, health, and family.

❖ Gina & Christopher – A warm loving fireside oasis on a bitterly cold NY night!

- ❖ Quayshawn – The biggest heart of anyone I know…helping me tarp the tent for the cold, money for food, checking up on us, and the purest friendship for my family. You are amazing young man and deserve the best that life has to offer!

- ❖ Bryan – You kept us on the move and the car running – that was priceless!

- ❖ Radika & Ricardo – Our secret chef's! The food was amazing fireside and our emergency storage!

- ❖ Patty & Brianna - There are no words to capture just how much you helped us, from driving the kids to school, a place to hang out, anything we needed!

- ❖ Sue, Krysta, & Neil – You will forever be the snow storm troopers!

Notes:

_____

_____

_____

_____

_____

_____

_____

_____

_____

_____

_____

_____

_____

_____

_____

_____

_____

_____

_____

_____

_____

_____

_____

_____

_____

_____

_____

_____

_____

_____

References

https://psy-minds.com/isis-goddess/

https://www.huffpost.com/entry/goddesses-from-around-the-world_n_56b8f607e4b08069c7a852d1

https://www.ancienthistorylists.com/greek-history/top-10-ancient-greek-goddesses/

https://www.indiebound.org/book/9781591432074

https://thetempest.co/2016/10/05/culture-taste/23-kickass-female-goddesses/

https://www.learnreligions.com/gods-and-goddesses-of-healing-2561980

https://greekgodsandgoddesses.net/goddesses/nike/

https://witchesofthecraft.com/2018/08/13/pagan-studies-of-the-gods-and-goddesses-maat-the-ancient-egyptian-goddess/

http://www.orderwhitemoon.org/goddess/oya-storms/Oya.html

https://www.webmd.com

https://www.acefitness.org/education-and-resources/lifestyle/blog/6468/carb-cycling

https://www.scientificamerican.com

https://www.britannica.com/science

https://www.healthline.com

https://www.mayoclinic.org

Made in the USA
Middletown, DE
30 June 2023

34272137R00050